Diggers

Monica Hughes

OXFORD
UNIVERSITY PRESS

bucket

This is a big digger.

wheels

It has a bucket and wheels.

scoop

This is a small digger.

track

It has a scoop and tracks.

bucket

This is a big digger.

scoop

It has a bucket and a scoop.

blade

This digger has a big blade.

It can dig in the snow.

arm

This digger has a long arm.

It can dig up mud.

This digger has a long arm.

12

arm

It can dig up rocks.

drill

This digger has a drill.

It can dig up the road.

arm

blade

bucket

drill

scoop

tracks

wheels

16